The Lost Art of Excellence

The Supernatural Character of Christ

Daniel T. Newton

© Copyright 2023 Daniel Newton, GP Publishing

www.GracePlaceRedding.com

Contributing authors: Downing McDade, Austin Chappell, Daniel Fagot, Katherine Marx, Elizabeth Newton, and the Grace Place Leadership Team
ISBN: 978-1-957601-08-3

"But since you excel in everything—in faith, in speech, in knowledge, in complete earnestness and in the love we have kindled in you—see that you also excel in this grace of giving."

- 2 Corinthians 8:7

Table of Contents

Introduction

Everyone's "normal" is different. Many things we consider to be "normal" are a direct result of the people and experiences that influenced us growing up. Our values and standards are almost always a reflection of those we look up to or surround ourselves with the most. While this impacts us greatly, the majority of people don't take the time to acknowledge it. Most go through life completely unaware of what or who is influencing them. Even if you grew up in a Christian home, it's easy for God to become nothing more than your Sunday duty. His values don't become your own, and He's nothing more than a topic of discussion.

For this reason, it's possible to glide through life without allowing Christ's standard to become your "normal." You have to take the time to consciously *choose* your standard of living. Otherwise, life happens to you—you don't happen to it.

I grew up in a great family. My parents were faith-filled, passionate lovers of God. Whenever there was news of a minister coming into the area, we would all jump into the car and drive—sometimes for hours—to go see him or her. My mom discipled younger women, occasionally bringing them in to live with us for a period of time. There were even times my dad would roll down his car window at stoplights and preach the Gospel to the people in the next car over. My parents constantly emulated a healthy Christian life. Their lifestyle left a lasting impression on my heart and mind, and because of it, I see the value of being raised well.

I realize that not everyone has that kind of story. I have discipled hundreds of people over the past twenty years. I've heard countless stories from men and women whose pasts were nothing like my own. Some lived through absolute hell. It's given me a passion for sharing with others the godly example my parents gave me. I want to give young men and women a model for healthy living. I want to show the world the fullness of living in Christ.

At some point or another, all of us will find an area of our lives where our standard falls below the standard of Christ. There's nothing wrong with discovering that. What really matters is what you do with this realization. The very reason Christ died for you was to deliver you from the power that sin and compromise had in your life.

All of us need to be open to the journey of being matured by the Lord, allowing His Word to prune and transform every part of our hearts. We all start in different places, but life is not about where you begin. It's about what you become despite where you began. In Christ, each of us finds the underserved opportunity to become what we could never be on our own.

There is so much more available in Christ than an ordinary human life. In fact, we were never made to be ordinary; we were made to be *excellent*. Excellence is one of the highest and best qualities of the character of God manifested in the lives of believers. Jesus Christ is excellence personified. We are called to follow Him.

Introduction

This book's message is one that some of you may not immediately like. Others of you will love reading it! For those of you who don't, I hope that you will grow to love it. I'm going to be honest with you. This is a challenging message, yet it's something I believe is vital to live out. It has great potential to refine and sharpen the Body of Christ, enabling Her to embrace a lifestyle worthy of Her calling.

People often wonder why this topic isn't talked about much, and I believe it's because it's very correctional. It's difficult to hear. Why? Because most of us don't live in excellence. It's convicting when you're confronted with something you know you're not living in. It's not fun to hear a message and be left thinking, "Wow...that's a far cry from who I am today."

The message of excellence is not supposed to make you feel condemned. This is a message of identity. It's a call for you to rise up and be the person God has made you to be. It's time for all of us to be the sons and daughters of God that the earth is groaning and longing for (see Rom. 8:22). We have to get to a place where we're walking out what He paid for. He did not pay for us to live a mediocre lifestyle. Nor did He sacrifice Himself so that we could run after the things of the world. He didn't die for us to keep sin in our lives. He paid for us to be completely free and to walk in excellence.

Excellence is the character of Christ manifested and embodied. It's the purity, simplicity, and integrity of His nature expressed in and through your daily activities and decisions. It is one of my most deeply held core values. If you come from a strong culture of grace that teaches, "I have been co-crucified. It is finished. I'm a new creation," you may be tempted to think what I'm teaching in this book is legalistic.

However, excellence is not the law. The law will never produce excellence at the heart level. True excellence is fueled by a transformed life that has embraced Jesus' empowerment to overcome compromise. Everything I'll say within these pages will challenge what you think it means to be a Christian. When you gave up your life to receive His, you gave up your right to define your life as anything other than "in Christ."

Your righteousness is found in Christ alone. Your purity is found in Christ alone. Your holiness is found in Christ alone. This book is meant to help you access another aspect of His grace that you may not yet be walking in. It will empower you to repent of and overcome laziness, irresponsibility, and lack of character and use grace as a license to live a complacent lifestyle (all of which can happen if we don't hold excellence as a core value).

This book is not meant to make you ashamed of areas where you find your values are misaligned with Jesus. Instead, I want to create an opportunity for all of us to see the places where we can become more like Him. The life of Jesus challenges us to live excellently in everything we do.

Excellence is a core value that I have taught to those in my ministry and in many churches around the world. As you read, do it with a determination to depend on Christ, and watch as the truths in this book infuse you with His grace. This will empower you to live by the standard He modeled when He walked the earth.

Chapter One

Called to His Excellence

When I first started Grace Place Ministries, I often asked God to bring me professionals. I would pray, "Lord, I need the best of the best to partner with me so I can share the Gospel of Jesus Christ and disciple the nations to the best of my ability."

This sounds like a valid prayer, right? However, in time, I realized something. When He walked the earth, Jesus didn't work with professionals. He *raised* professionals. No one is born perfect. There's never been a doctor born with a degree nor a scientist born with his or her credentials already in hand. People become professionals by embracing their journey and giving their best. That's why when the world looked at Jesus' disciples, they were in awe. They saw a group of men from all walks of life who *became* something by spending time around Jesus.

"Now when they saw the boldness of Peter and John, and perceived that they were uneducated and untrained men, they marveled. And they realized that they had been with Jesus."

- Acts 4:13

Why am I telling you this? Because I want to set the record straight that any person, no matter where they come from or what they know, can excel to unimaginable heights. Grace Place Ministries has been an example to me of this principle for more than 13 years. I am constantly blown away by the creativity and excellence of my leadership team. It's all because they continue to embrace this straightforward but essential truth:

"His divine power has granted to us everything pertaining to life and godliness, through the true knowledge of Him who called us by His own glory and excellence."
- 2 Peter 1:3 (NASB)

We are called into excellence, and His divine grace empowers us into godliness. Everything we do becomes worship. Nothing is mundane when Christ is at the center of our lives. When you understand that He died for you so that you could live for Him, your perspective goes from "just getting by" to excelling, achieving, and becoming everything you can be in order to honor the One who gave it all. As we develop a passion for excellence, we draw on God's abundant grace to live it out.

"And whatever you do, do it heartily, as to the Lord and not to men."
- Colossians 3:23

Everything you put your hands to is meant to exhibit God's excellence. Are you at home doing chores? Make that house the cleanest it's ever been! Are you hosting a barbecue for a youth group? Make it the best barbecue those kids have ever had! Are you stuck at a job you don't like? Ask God to show you

His perspective and why He has you there. Serve with all your heart in worship to God because, ultimately, that's exactly what your life is: worship! You're either worshiping God, or you're worshiping your desires, your problems, your doubts, and your circumstances.

Take ownership of what you have in front of you now, and God will take you into bigger and better places. Whether you're doing something you don't like or something you love, embrace the mindset that you are there for a reason. Everything you do has a purpose. You're right where you are today to show the world what the character of Christ looks like.

"Therefore, whether you eat or drink, or whatever you do,
do all to the glory of God."
- 1 Corinthians 10:31

Made to Excel

Have you ever watched a Christian film and thought to yourself, "Well, that was good for a *Christian* movie!"

What are we telling ourselves? Are Christian films supposed to be graded on a curve? If something is produced by a Spirit-filled man or woman, shouldn't we expect it to excel far beyond what the world is creating? However, we've told ourselves that we are held back by small budgets and limited resources. Do you understand how deeply this mentality has been adopted by the Church as a whole?

Most Christians have failed to take their rightful place in the world as ambassadors of God's Kingdom who reveal His abundance, excellence, and majesty. As a believer, everything you put your hands to is meant to prosper. It's not meant to be "good enough." It's meant to surpass the world's understanding of what "good" even is. The Spirit of the living God is within you, which means you're capable of transcending every worldly idea, perspective, and invention. The Church has lost touch with the creative substance of God's nature.

Why is mainstream media overrun with wickedness? Why are the most prominent inventors and wealthiest people not those within the Church? Because the Church has been brainwashed to clench her teeth, dig her heels in, and wait until she gets to heaven someday. This escapist mentality has robbed believers of their inheritance and created an apathetic culture within the Body of Christ. One might ask, "What are you waiting for?" An all-too-predictable reply would be, "I'm just waiting for the rapture, brother. We're all going to be going home real soon." Stop waiting! Every day can be a rapture in His love and goodness! Heaven is eagerly waiting to inspire people with mind-bending solutions and supernatural ideas, but we will never receive them if we are just living to die and go to heaven. It's time to excel. It's time to truly live!

"But just as you excel in everything, in faith, speech, knowledge, and in all earnestness and in the love we inspired in you, see that you also excel in this gracious work."

- 2 Corinthians 8:7

The best architects should be the men and women of God who have received blueprints from heaven. The best musicians should be the creators who have heard the songs of angels. The best inventors should be those who have communed face-to-face with the Creator Himself. This is what it means to be excellent:

to excel and reveal the fullness of God's multi-dimensional goodness to the world! We cannot afford to accept defeat in this area. It's time to arise and shine.

Every reality in our lives is an overflow of our hearts. As it says in Matthew 12:35, "A good man out of the good treasure of his heart brings forth good things, and an evil man out of the evil treasure brings forth evil things." As you excel in kindness, humility, and love from within your heart, you will find that your character will prepare a place for you that you could never achieve in your own strength.

It doesn't take a fight to live in the heart posture of excellence. Someone who understands excellence understands their value, regardless of what they have put their hands to. They understand that there would be something lacking if they weren't present. When you have this mindset in the small, menial tasks, you will find yourself naturally upgraded to higher positions of influence. Steward your talents well, and God will give you cities (see Luke 19:12-27).

Prosperity and Excellence

Prosperity may not be the goal of excellence. It is, however, the near inevitable result of it. If you value excellent things, you will be drawn to what people in the Church may consider "glamorous" or "too much." But, someone who understands excellence won't settle for less when they know Jesus died to give them more.

This doesn't mean you avoid the discomforts that may come with persecution; it means you know how to enjoy God's provision as one of His sons or daughters. Many people in the

Church today live in a state of poverty in the name of "taking up their cross" or "suffering for the Gospel." All the while, they are actually self-sabotaging God's goodness in their lives. God didn't bankrupt heaven for you to scrape by. He sent His Son so you could have authority in this life and freely inherit all things. (Read more about this in my book *All Things*.)

"For you know the grace of our Lord Jesus Christ, that though He was rich, yet for your sakes He became poor, so that you through His poverty might become rich."
-2 Corinthians 8:9

Having nice things isn't wrong—it's *godly*. Being blessed is a byproduct of putting your faith in the power of the Cross. As you grow in this journey of excellence, I would encourage you not to allow mindsets of lack and poverty to creep in and rob you of advancing to the place God wants you. Abundance is your portion. It's not about what you own—it's about what owns *you*. As you grow in believing His goodness toward you, countless blessings will come. I encourage you to receive them with open arms, knowing that God has called you into a rich inheritance.

"He who did not spare His own Son, but delivered Him up for us all, how shall He not with Him also freely give us all things?"
- Romans 8:32

Chapter Two

Relevant or Excellent?

"Let no one despise your youth, but be an example to the believers in word, in conduct, in love, in spirit, in faith, in purity."

- 1 Timothy 4:12

Isn't it alarming how much of the world's culture has spread into the Church? And it's happened in the name of being "relevant." So often, I hear, "Well, we're trying to be relevant to the world." What does that mean? Last time I checked, the Bible says that we're *in* the world but not *of* it (see Rom. 12:2, 1 John 2:15, John 15:19, John 17:14-18) and that we're called to be a light in the world's darkest places (see Matt. 5:14-16). We're not called to say, "Oh, I can look like darkness as well." We're called to stand out. We're called to be an example in our speech and in our conduct. We're called to be an example through our love. We're called to be an example of faith. We're called to be an example of purity.

There's so much pressure being put on us to conform to the mindsets, ideologies, and trends of the world. It's tempting to give in when it feels like that's the only way to "fit in." Did you know that a large percentage of young people raised in Christian homes walk away from their faith when they go to college? They get into the world, and because they aren't secure in their identity, they try to prove themselves to gain acceptance.

However, you won't have anything to prove when you know you are loved, valued, and treasured by God. You've been approved by the Creator Himself! Many of us are unsure of ourselves and insecure. Because of this, we often attempt to garner self-value by proving ourselves to other people. This only leaves us lost in a confusing and unending maze of performance.

We need to come back to the simplicity and purity of the Gospel. We are loved, we are holy, and we are His. We need to restore the standard of the Early Church rather than being conformed to this world (see Rom. 12:1-2).

Counterfeit Standards

Sixty years ago, they wouldn't go so far as to show a man and a woman sleeping in the same bed on television. Today, television is saturated with impurity. Our entertainment is filled with things that would have been considered perverse and inappropriate a generation ago. Is it possible that the Church's standard has lowered because of how passive we've become? Is it possible that as the world has gotten worse, the Church's culture has followed suit?

For example, how on earth is it ever okay for Christians to think it's funny to make or entertain crude and sexual jokes? Yet, I travel all over the world and hear it all the time from Christians—the ones called and chosen to represent Jesus on the earth! What happened? We gave in to a system, to worldly culture, and we didn't choose to live excellently. We decided to laugh at something that lowered our standards, and we slowly began to look more like the world around us.

"Do not conform to the pattern of this world, but be transformed by the renewing of your mind. Then you will be able to test and approve what God's will is—his good, pleasing and perfect will."
– Romans 12:2 (NIV)

How many of you have ever met a con artist? If you've ever met one, they're not stupid. They would never con a person who is broke. They are opportunists looking to get the most for their efforts. No one counterfeits $1 bills. Why? Because they are not worth much. What do counterfeiters duplicate? The $100 bills. Why? Because they're the most valuable.

Why do you think the world has become so saturated with immorality, pornography, homosexuality, crude and sexual humor, and all these filthy, perverse things? Because the enemy is not stupid, and he knows that sexuality and purity actually hold immense value. So, what is he going to do? He's going to counterfeit, imitate, and pervert it. In short, he's going to try to offer you something that looks good and feels good but ultimately leaves you bankrupt.

Unfortunately, we buy into this all the time. Through desensitization to sin, the enemy gets us comfortable with compromise. When we sacrifice the standard at which we live our lives, we lose our edge and influence in the world. "You are the salt of the earth; but if the salt loses its flavor, how shall it be seasoned? It is then good for nothing but to be thrown out and trampled underfoot by men" (Matt. 5:13). If we lose our saltiness and become comfortable with compromise, we do not show the earth Christ's standard of excellence and holiness.

How do we lose our value for excellence? It happens gradually. Whenever we laugh at something that isn't true, holy, or excellent, we slowly become desensitized to it. After some time, it becomes acceptable. Jesus wouldn't be laughing at crude jokes. Yet I hear it and see it everywhere, and I think to myself, *How is that acceptable for us as the Church*? The first step of desensitizing our minds to sin is making it into a joke.

In the late '90s, homosexuality was aired on television with a few distinct public figures openly owning it as part of their lifestyle. Soon after, movies and TV shows began making fun of LGBTQ people. Throughout the comedic community, people would call each other "homos." Slowly but surely, the concept of homosexuality leaked into our movies, TV shows, books, and entertainment. While it was first presented in a joking manner, it then began to transition into minor roles within shows.

Nowadays, it is almost unheard of to have a TV show that does not have a character from the LGBTQ community. In fact, the LGBTQ community is strongly defended and justified in their lifestyle choice by the masses. If you voice a dissenting opinion to them, it's quickly labeled as "hate speech."

There are many people, not just in the world but in the Church also, whose hearts and minds have become defiled and polluted because they've taken on things that are not excellent. They've taken on things that are not even good. They've taken on mediocre things. They've taken on wrong things. And they've settled for living a worldly life.

"Let each of you look out not only for his own interests, but also for the interests of others. Let this mind be in you which was also in Christ Jesus..."
– Philippians 2:4-5

Again I'll say it: We were never called to be relevant. People say, "you're so heavenly-minded that you're no earthly good." That makes no sense! We are called to be full of heaven! That phrase is a slap in the face to our calling in Christ. We are citizens and ambassadors of heaven. When you are heavenly-minded, you are earthly-good by default. Jesus was full of heaven and brought freedom and transformation everywhere He went, casting out demons, healing the sick, and raising the dead. If we truly bring heaven everywhere we go, everything will be transformed around us.

Reverence Over Relevance

"The fear of the Lord is the beginning of wisdom."
- Proverbs 9:10

The only fear we should make room for in our lives is the fear of God. We need to rise above our fear of what people think and say to fully express the nature of Christ. If we are limited by the fear of man, we will have difficulty looking like God. Paul was the perfect example of someone who desired reverence over relevance. He would go into cities knowing he would be hated, attacked, and beaten. He wasn't looking for relevance. He wanted to see transformation.

Can you imagine having this mindset? Can you imagine being so strong in Christ and God's identity that any human's judgments against you won't move you? That is our calling. Out of reverence for the Maker of every living thing, we should always aim to excel, give our best, and be conformed to the image of His Son.

"Keep your behavior excellent among the Gentiles, so that in the thing in which they slander you as evildoers, they may because of your good deeds, as they observe them, glorify God in the day of visitation."
- 1 Peter 2:12

Many today say that the best way to minister to the world is to look like them, talk like them, laugh at the things they laugh at, and do the things they do. Cultural "relevance" has become the norm. The thought seems to be something along the lines of "If we look or sound too 'churchy,' no one's going to want to be a part of us." However, this scripture says that what is most attractive to the lost is seeing the good deeds you do. They may slander you or publicly show no interest, but behind the scenes, they are watching, and they are curious.

For this reason, Peter says to keep your behavior excellent among the Gentiles (unbelievers). Because "as they observe them," they glorify God. If all we ever do is act like unbelievers, talk like unbelievers, and do what unbelievers do, how will they ever see anything different from what they already have? To be clear, unbelievers don't need to see your church programs or guest speaker lineup. First, they need to see you!

"Let your light so shine before men, that they may see your good works, and glorify your Father which is in heaven."
– Matthew 5:16

Your good deeds should give people a reason to praise God. But if you're caught up in compromise or don't "feel convicted" by committing sinful actions, what will they see that gives them a reason to glorify God? Jesus says that you shouldn't be ashamed of following Him in front of people. Don't worry about what they think and don't worry about being different. We're not called to stoop to the low standards of the world; we're called to demonstrate the reality that comes through knowing Jesus.

Chapter Three

Excellence in Scripture

"There is a way that seems right to a man, But its end is the way of death."
- Proverbs 14:12

Think about the first time you used the Internet. Most likely, you were introduced to it through your parents, a teacher, or possibly even a professional. You were introduced to an entirely new system that allowed you to access information at an unprecedented rate, and it used a completely different mode of communication than you might have been used to. You weren't talking to a person to get information. You were getting it from your computer screen. When I was growing up, you would spend hours going to the library, searching for the proper book, and thumbing through pages to find the information you need. But now, you could find what you were looking for with a few keystrokes.

In the same way that someone taught you how to interact with this new world called "the Internet," you also needed someone to teach you about God. You needed a spokesperson who would condense the vast array of God's nature into something material, understandable, and human.

In comes Jesus. Jesus came to be the exact representation of what God looked like, how He thought, and what He wanted (see Heb. 1:3). Jesus' life shows that God did not require man to come to Him through his own efforts. He took on our human condition so that we might know Him in our own context. God Himself is spirit, but He became flesh so we could experience what He's like. He didn't have a selfish motive. He lived a life completely laid down to the point of dying on the Cross so that He could save us and have a relationship with us. By doing this, He showed us what a life of excellence looks like. Later in this book, I will address more practical applications of excellence, but the cornerstone of the message of excellence is found in 2 Peter 1.

"For His divine power has bestowed upon us all things that [are requisite and suited] to life and godliness, through the [full, personal] knowledge of Him Who called us by and to His own glory and excellence (virtue). By means of these He has bestowed on us His precious and exceedingly great promises, so that through them you may escape [by flight] from the moral decay (rottenness and corruption) that is in the world because of covetousness (lust and greed), and become sharers (partakers) of the divine nature."

- 2 Peter 1:3-4 (AMPC)

He called us by and to His own glory and excellence. He lived, loved, died, and rose again so that we might know Him. Other than reconciling us back as His beloved, nothing that Jesus did was for His own gain. If you try to live excellently to get the respect of others, seem holy, or add to your own influence, you will find yourself constantly falling short of the goal set for us in Jesus' life. The only way to live excellently is to lay down your life and realize that you are no longer your own. The moment you said "Yes" to Jesus, you gave up the right you had to live for yourself and your desires. You signed your life away, and now you have His.

Now that you have given Him your life, He wants to live His life through you! Any portion of your life that is not living in the standard of excellence according to Scripture is an area you can surrender to Christ. Sometimes, these parts of our lives are not easily recognized. We can go a long time without knowing we have settled in an area. Or, perhaps we have become prideful and assumed that our understanding and expectations determine how we will live instead of Christ's.

God may bring these things up through Scripture or lead us to surrender them in our time with Him. He also uses strong, mature, Christian leaders in our lives to call us higher. What ultimately matters is how we respond to His conviction. Excellence remains a lost art when we reject God's correction, whether through the Word or someone else.

Why Confrontation Matters

I want to encourage you to expand your mind: The next time you're confronted by your pastor, a leader, or a family member and you don't initially agree, ask yourself, "I don't see what they are saying, but could I be wrong?" It *seems* right. It *looks* right. It *feels* right.

We should think, *Wait a second. Why is this person telling me this? Could it be possible that I have a blind spot? Could it be possible that they see something that I don't?* We should question ourselves instead of shutting down, putting a wall up, and saying, "No, I don't want to hear it." In the end, that's self-preservation, and it's self-centered.

You might say, "Well, I don't think it's wrong." To be frank, I could care less if you think it's right or wrong. The question is, is it excellent? The moment you got saved, your life was given to the One who is excellent. Jesus takes you deeper than right vs. wrong or good vs. bad. He raises the standard. He doesn't lower it.

We can ask ourselves, *Does the fruit of my character empower those around me? Do my actions give life? Do they honor God and man?* The moment you were saved and born again, you gave up your right to do wrong, so wrong should never be in the equation.

We began this chapter with Proverbs 14:12, which says, "There is a way that seems right to a man, but its end is the way of death." Reread this and think about what it is saying. There is a way that looks right, feels right, and seems right. You might even have people tell you it is right. But the truth is, if you looked at your action according to Scripture, you would find it's wrong. Ultimately, it doesn't matter how good something looks, feels, seems, or sounds. If it isn't right according to the truth, its way will lead you toward death.

God wants what is best for you, but sometimes we get to the place where we don't want what's best for ourselves. Instead of repenting and changing how we think and behave, we try to hold onto our preferences and habits. I can't tell you how many times in my twenty-plus years of ministry I've heard people say things like:

"Well, I'm not convicted about that."

"That's not a big deal to me."

"God's not speaking to me about this, so, obviously, I'm okay to do it."

"Well, we all have different convictions."

"Well, I don't go to church anymore...I don't agree with this."

"No one is speaking into my life. I have Jesus."

Meanwhile, I'm thinking, *How do you not see that what you're doing is wrong?* Just because you feel you have a justification for doing something doesn't mean your actions are justified. What seems right to you is standing in the way of what is actually right. What you need isn't a better excuse to keep doing what you're doing but to repent of your old way of thinking and adjust the lens you see through.

Many people want to avoid confrontation altogether because of how they react to it or how it makes them feel. However, there's never a time when we should feel guilty and condemned when confronted. I'm not saying that feeling bad for something you've done wrong is a poor response. That can be godly sorrow, which always leads to repentance. However, if you are dragged down into a navel-gazing, sin-conscious life, you will become unproductive and altogether unfruitful.

"Godly sorrow brings repentance that leads to salvation and leaves no regret, but worldly sorrow brings death."
- 2 Corinthians 7:10 (NIV)

If you notice, most people tend to live in one extreme or the other in this area of their life. You find pride, arrogance, and independence on one side: "Well, I don't really see anything wrong with that. I don't have a problem with that. That's your conviction, not mine. Yeah, that's not a big deal to me."

On the other side, you have condemnation, shame, and guilt: "I'm a wicked, evil sinner. I am horrible, and everything around me is a mess, etc." These are two polarizing mindsets. So what's in the middle? Humility. The humility to rightly apply the Word of God to your life.

The more open and humble-hearted you are with your leaders and the Lord, the more you will receive correction and redirection. This will cause you to grow and, ultimately, look like Jesus.

Most of us make decisions without taking the time to think about how the way we carry ourselves today will affect tomorrow. However in five to ten years, when you're a husband or wife, when you're a father or mother, when you own a business, or are leading a ministry, the small decisions you made today will have a major impact on the lives around you. I'm not living for the here and now. I'm living for legacy and for future generations.

We all love encouragement, and it definitely has its place. However five years from now, if you take the amount of encouragement that you received versus the amount of healthy confrontation you received, which do you think would have caused the most growth? Confrontation. What is encouragement going to do? It's going to make you feel good. It's going to confirm your calling and edify you as a believer. Encouragement can be beneficial if it helps you step into God's purposes for you. However, if encouragement leads you to be comfortable with immaturity in your life, it has stopped being beneficial. That's where confrontation is needed to call you higher.

When you see an area that might need growth, ask the Lord: "Is this something I need to work on? Is this something I need to change?" Check yourself when you're being confronted. Are you defensive? Do your walls go up? If so, there's a problem, and it most likely lies in the way you perceive confrontation. Remember, the person that's confronting you cares about you. They love you enough to call you higher.

Some people think I enjoy confronting others. However, to be honest, after 20 years of discipleship, I still don't like confronting people. What I enjoy is the outcome of them walking into their God-given potential and the connection it brings. However, it is still not initially enjoyable to have those hard conversations. There are plenty of other ways I would rather spend my time, but I am not making the decision to confront based on how I feel. Rather, it's about the growth of the other person. It is always rewarding to see the fruit in the lives of those I lead and confront. In reality, those I love the most and am closest to receive the most correction. Confrontation done healthily is always a sign of value for the person being confronted. You wouldn't confront someone that you don't care about. You confront them because you believe in them.

Excellence in the Word

It is vital to understand the proper way to respond when you are challenged. Why? Scripture calls us to a lifestyle that is challenging! For the rest of this chapter, we'll look more directly at what the Bible teaches about excellence and God's intended design for us. I'm going to use plenty of scriptures. This may seem very challenging to you. I would encourage you to keep an open heart in the pages to come. Apply what you've read so far and prepare your mind to accept and embrace what the Lord wants to speak to you through these verses.

"Now for this very reason also, applying all diligence, in your faith supply moral excellence, and in your moral excellence, knowledge, and in your knowledge, self-control, and in your self-control, perseverance, and in your perseverance, godliness, and in your godliness, brotherly kindness, and in your brotherly kindness, love. For if these qualities are yours and are increasing, they do not make you useless nor unproductive in the true knowledge of our Lord Jesus Christ. For the one who lacks these qualities is blind or short-sighted, having forgotten his purification from his former sins."

- 2 Peter 1:5-9 (NASB)

Notice what this passage says about those who lack these qualities. They lack them not because they have never been told or trained but because they have *forgotten*. You might ask, "Forgotten what?" The verse goes on:

"...that you have been purified from your former sins."

Peter is saying that knowing and remembering the mercy and forgiveness that the Father released to you in your conversion actually safeguards you from becoming unfruitful in your life. The question isn't whether or not we have been forgiven and purified but whether or not we have held to the knowledge that we have been forgiven and purified. This is crucial to living an excellent life as a believer.

Our hearts can become blind when we fail to hold fast to the Gospel. When lies from the enemy, worldly wisdom, wrong feelings, or past experiences seek to undermine our confidence, we must decide to stand firm on the promise of our salvation. Otherwise, we allow the voice of the world to become more clear and the truth to become harder and harder to see and grasp. In other words, we become short-sighted. It doesn't happen all at once but slowly, over time, as we surrender more ground to the enemy's work in our lives. We must remain aware of the subtle strategies of the enemy that fight to remove us from our posture of excellence toward God. This awareness empowers us to resist the darkness and choose God's way consistently.

There are eight qualities Peter lists that are true to the nature of the believer. They are faith, moral excellence, knowledge, self-control, perseverance, godliness, brotherly kindness, and love. However, the character of short-sightedness is doubt, moral mediocrity, ignorance, instability, laziness, worldliness, callousness, and fear. No one becomes like this overnight, but the more you compromise or let go of your godly confidence in order to please the world, each of these traits will gradually make its way into your life.

Chosen for His Excellence

"But you are a chosen people, a royal priesthood, a holy nation, a people for God's own possession, so that you may proclaim the excellencies of Him who has called you out of darkness into His marvelous light..."
- 1 Peter 2:9 (NASB)

You didn't choose to believe in God by accident. Every event that led to your conversion was divinely orchestrated. Before the foundations of the world, He desired you and chose you to be redeemed and to become a part of Himself through Jesus. You are not an accident. You were chosen by Him. It's so important that we understand this because it means that no matter what happens to us in life, we are desired and wanted by God. But what were we chosen for? What were we called to be?

In the passage above, Peter teaches that we are called to be three things: a chosen people, a royal priesthood, and a holy nation. We should live our lives in such a way that when people look at us as believers, they see the One we belong to. Our lifestyles and interactions with others are meant to reveal something about God. He took us out of the darkness and brought us into His marvelous light. This shows that we live in the same light that He lives in. 1 John 1:5 says that God is light, and in Him is no darkness. So, if we see an area of our life where we are still comfortable living in or desiring the darkness of the world, it's an area where our minds need to be renewed to the truth.

"Therefore, my beloved brothers, be steadfast, immovable, always abounding in the work of the Lord, knowing that in the Lord your labor is not in vain."
- 1 Corinthians 15:58 (ESV)

One key partner to the life of excellence is steadfastness. Oftentimes, we become reliant on the immediate result. If we do something right but don't see transformation soon enough, we get discouraged. We need to break our addiction to "microwave Christianity," or instant gratification. Remember the heroes of the faith. They embraced longsuffering with their eyes on the promises to come. Persist in faith, and you will see the result of your daily decisions to walk in excellence.

Think about Noah, who spent 100 years building a big wooden boat for a storm that no one had ever seen or believed was possible. In his day, water came from the ground and not in the form of rain. The people of his time were convinced that

Noah was crazy, but Noah knew the Lord was faithful to His Word. He remained steadfast (see Gen. 6-7).

We do not live a life of excellence because we are looking for a certain result. Rather, we live excellently because we are here to manifest Christ and follow His example to bring glory to the Father. The Lord is a just judge in all that He does, and He is aware of the little corners you choose not to cut. He sees the good works that you do. Each action you take in His character will magnify His name in the earth.

"Therefore, whether you eat or drink, or whatever you do, do all to the glory of God."
- 1 Corinthians 10:31

Whatever you are doing, you are doing it for the Lord. Our reward is bringing glory to Him as we abide with Him in every moment, obeying His commands. What is His chief command? To love Him and love others. Loving Him looks like trusting Him enough to live in obedience, surrendering our daily decisions and very lives to Him in love. Loving others looks like honoring and preferring them above ourselves. You are not cleaning your room just to follow your parents' or spouse's request. You aren't finishing menial tasks at work just because your boss asked you to do them. You are doing this unto the Lord. No one can top His standard. In fact, He is the standard. As He leads you and guides you, you will see that people no longer have to micromanage you because you have developed an internal system of excellence that relies on God's voice and His standards.

"But since you excel in everything—in faith, in speech, in knowledge, in complete earnestness and in the love we have kindled in you —see that you also excel in this grace of giving."

-2 Corinthians 8:7 (NIV)

When Paul wrote to the Corinthians, he wrote in order to bring correction and guidance. If we are not careful, we can overlook the language that Paul uses when establishing a standard. In 2 Corinthians 8:7, he writes, "But since you excel in everything..." He does not say, "Now that you are doing pretty well," or "Now that you're just a bit better than the world..." He makes it clear that the standard is excelling in all things. In Christ, we are to come out and be separate, living holy and set apart to Him. Without holiness and blamelessness, the world will not see God.

When a parent gives boundaries to a young child, it's often humorous to watch how close they try to get without actually breaking them. For example, if the parent says that the child can play in the front yard, but the boundary is to stay off the street, you might see them walking along the curb. The same thought is present in the Church today. Somewhere it got into our heads that maturity in the Christian life looks like being able to play as close to the boundaries without falling into sin.

We treat life like a game of limbo. *How low can I go without actually falling?* This isn't excellence. This isn't living above reproach. This is trying to do just enough to make it. People live this way and then come to me when they sin, confused as to why they can't seem to break free. Living blamelessly is the fruit of living excellently, not living in what we can manage to get away with.

For example, if you have struggled with sexual purity in the past, living with a high standard may look like deciding not to be in the same room alone with a person of the opposite sex. It would not look like justifying borderline behavior by saying, "Oh, I've grown so much since two months ago. I'm ready to spend time alone with my girlfriend now!" That would be neither wise nor excellent. This thinking leads you to compromise through a slow process of justifying, gradually letting go of any firm conviction you hold.

"And may the Lord make you increase and abound in love to one another and to all, just as we do to you, so that He may establish your hearts blameless in holiness before our God and Father at the coming of our Lord Jesus Christ with all His saints."
– 1 Thessalonians 3:12-13

Jesus said that He had given a new commandment: to love each other as He has loved us (see John 13:34). There is no greater love than a man who lays down His life for His friend (see John 15:13). The love that Jesus lavished on us was not second-rate. It was not a partial representation of the riches of heaven. Christ poured out His life for us while we were still His enemies. That is the ultimate revelation of excellence. If we live our lives focused on ourselves and how we can achieve worldly success, we will never know the depths of His mercy and grace. The blameless nature of Christ inspires us to love and live excellently toward all people. The goal of the Christian life is to look like Christ in all we do. Everything He did was excellent.

"To the pure [in heart and conscience] all things are pure..."
- Titus 1:15 (AMPC)

I've heard people say inappropriate and impure things before, and I've confronted them by asking, "Is that acceptable to you?" They sometimes reply, "Daniel, to the pure, all things are pure. So, it doesn't matter. Because I've been made pure, I can say anything or look at anything and call it pure!" Wow! What a way to bend the scripture!

Matthew 12:34 says, "For out of the abundance of the heart the mouth speaks." If your heart and conscience were really pure, would you speak impurities? If you were really pure, would you want to make space for something vile in your life?

What this verse is really saying is that your life is a reflection of the condition of your heart. To someone whose heart is pure and desiring to please the Lord, their life will reflect this. Everything around them becomes a sign to point them back toward their love and connection to the Lord. Even the smallest things become confirmations of what the Lord is saying to them. They can walk into the darkest places in the world and find something pure and holy to point out because their hearts are looking for pure things. All things are pure for them. This is true of the other side as well:

"...but to those who are defiled and unbelieving nothing is pure;
their very minds and consciences are defiled and polluted."
- Titus 1:15 (AMPC)

Have you ever met someone who can make anything you say sound dirty and inappropriate? Where do those thoughts come from? If your heart is full of defilement and sin, you will see sin and defilement everywhere. Another translation says, "That person's mind and conscience are destroyed" (CEV). On the other hand, Matthew 6:22 says, "if the eye is single, the body will be filled with light." Be careful what you allow to influence your heart. As Proverbs 4:23 teaches, "Keep your heart with all diligence, for out of it spring the issues of life."

"Walk in the wisdom of God as you live before the unbelievers, and make it your duty to make Him known. Let every word you speak be drenched with grace and tempered with truth and clarity. For then you will be prepared to give a respectful answer to anyone who asks about your faith."

– Colossians 4:5-6 (TPT)

If you're so compromised in your convictions that you don't stand for anything, how will you be able to have an answer prepared for those who ask? If you live like the world, who will be asking about your faith at all? If you're compromised in your speech, allowing yourself to say whatever comes into your head, how will your words be drenched in grace and tempered with truth? If you live the same way as the unbelievers around you, how will you ever stand out and make Jesus known? Who will be able to see the wisdom of God manifesting in your life?

If the culture of the world is normal to you, then you will always end up looking like it. Your values will match the world's values. If you allow Jesus and His way of life to become your normal, your life will become transformed to match His. You will begin to live out the excellence that He walked in, and your life will be a testimony of His goodness. People will see you and wonder what is different about you. Your good works will glorify Him. The journey of transformation begins with the decision to change the way you think and what you meditate on. Make the decision to focus on the most excellent things so that they become a part of your everyday life.

> *"Finally, brethren, whatever things are true, whatever things are noble, whatever things are just, whatever things are pure, whatever things are lovely, whatever things are of good report, if there is any virtue and if there is anything praiseworthy— meditate on these things."*
>
> *– Philippians 4:8*

Chapter Four

Practical Excellence

One of the first times I was in South Africa, I was invited to preach at a school.

Somebody raised their hand and asked, "The Bible says I can't do this, this, and this. Well, why can't I?"

I said, "You're looking at the Word as a list of do's and don'ts. I don't look at it that way. I look at it and think, 'My loving Father is trying to protect me, and He's looking out for me. Because I know He loves me, I'm going to do what He tells me to do. I love Him, too, and know He has my best interest in mind.'"

You see, we turn our relationship with God into an obligation-based relationship. We say, "Oh well, I have to tithe. I have to serve. I have to do this. I have to do that." We end up forcing ourselves to do something when we really don't want to. This is nothing more than behavior modification. God has called us to live from the heart as we depend on Him. He is saying, "Listen, I'd rather you just rely on Me and let Me transform you." Take a look at these scriptures:

"For I desire mercy, not sacrifice, and acknowledgment of God rather than burnt offerings."
- Hosea 6:6 (NIV)

"You do not delight in sacrifice, or I would bring it; you do not take pleasure in burnt offerings."
- Psalm 51:16 (NIV)

"Therefore, when Christ came into the world, he said: "Sacrifice and offering you did not desire, but a body you prepared for me; with burnt offerings and sin offerings you were not pleased. Then I said, 'Here I am—it is written about me in the scroll— I have come to do your will, my God.'"
- Hebrews 10:5-7 (NIV)

The Word says He doesn't even want your sacrifice; He wants your love. He wants you. He wants your passion. He doesn't want your obligation. He wants you to *want* to do something. Anything done from obligation alone is a dead work or a work done without faith.

Everything you do, you should do for the glory of God. Even if you don't always feel like it, you're called to do everything for Him. Whether you're feeding a homeless person or meeting with the president, you're doing it for the glory of God. This must be embedded in your mind and heart. Every one of your actions done from this place will change how you think about people and circumstances.

Integrity

There is an old saying that goes, "The way you do one thing is the way you do all things." The Bible says it like this: "If you are faithful with little you will be faithful with much" (Luke 16:10). If you can't manage your temper with your family, you probably won't be able to control it when someone cuts you off in traffic or the grocery line. Living with integrity looks like being the same *you* no matter who's watching. Whether you're by yourself or on a stage before thousands, integrity empowers you to walk by Christ's standards.

You cannot expect to be recognized by others as being a person of excellence when you haven't practiced it in secret. Song of Solomon 2:15 says that the little foxes spoil the vine, meaning that it's the small, seemingly insignificant decisions that decide how fruitful our lives will be. Excellence has become a lost art because culture says the little foxes don't matter. However, living a life of excellence means addressing the little foxes. In this section, we are going to explore what excellence looks like in our everyday lives and what it means to be set apart in how we handle our personal responsibilities.

Your Word is Your Bond

"But let your 'Yes' be 'Yes,' and your 'No,' 'No.' For whatever is more than these is from the evil one."
- Matthew 5:37

Here is a big one: "Hey man, how are you doing? Good to see you! Let's hang out tomorrow, okay?" Then tomorrow comes, and you don't do anything or follow through on your word. Sadly, Church culture is notorious for this. It's as if people feel pressured to tell you that they want to connect, but then everyone is so busy that the intentions never become actions.

We have so many people that we run into all the time, and because we don't know how to manage ourselves well, we end up saying things we can't back up. "Hey, let's hang out sometime soon!" Did you mean that, or did you just need something nice to say? We end up making commitments we don't have any intention of fulfilling. We think about it later and say, "Why did I say that?" Then, we change our minds and decide not to do anything about it and wait for it to be forgotten. While this may be common, it's actually a decision to settle for a lack of integrity that ultimately causes us to become comfortable with compromise. Watering down the power of our word leads us to compromise in our standard of excellence.

Proverbs 20:25 says, "An impulsive vow is a trap; later you'll wish you could get out of it" (MSG). Don't give in to impulsiveness and allow yourself to give out an empty promise. Proverbs later says, "A person who promises a gift but doesn't give it is like clouds and wind that bring no rain" (Prov. 25:14). Your words and time are "gifts" that you give. If you promise them liberally but don't do anything to follow up, it's like a cloud and wind with no rain. You look like you're going to do something beneficial, but in the end, you just blow on by. It's time for us to take our word seriously. It's the bond we have with other people. It's the only way to let your "yes" really mean yes and your "no" really mean no!

When people say over and over that they want to hang out, but I know they are just saying it to be "nice," I'll just be honest with them. I say, "Hey, I know you're trying to be nice, but if you really want to connect, please follow through and let's actually make it happen." Invest in relationships you truly value and make the conscious choice to be intentional with them. You can't be intentional with a hundred people. It's impossible! Choose to invest in the relationships that matter to you. Don't tell people something you don't mean. Saying something that you don't mean isn't love—it's fake.

"Well, Daniel, I don't want them to feel bad." I'd rather have someone feel bad and know the truth than try to make them feel good by telling them something fake or false, which is lying. Conversely, I appreciate it when people tell me they're busy and that it might be a while before we get to do something together. It lets me know they value their time and that when they do say they'll be able to meet, I can trust their word. There are times I have to tell people, "I'm really sorry, but I don't have time." If it's the truth, there's nothing wrong with that. It may not make the person feel good in the moment, but telling the truth is always better than lying. Being able to make honest assessments of our capacity and communicate that to others is part of being a mature adult and living according to God's standard of excellence.

Time Management

Time management and integrity are extremely important. How do you manage your time? *Do you* manage your time, or do you let it manage you? When I hear people say they have difficulty turning things in on time or difficulty arriving on time, that tells me something is wrong in their life. Do you consistently run out of time to do your work? Do you often find yourself running out of money before the end of the month? Are you frequently late to engagements that you commit to? Do you find yourself setting goals but repeatedly falling short of them? Do you avoid making commitments because they make you feel boxed in? If you find yourself having hours a day to spend on social media, watch movies, and hang out with friends but not take care of what matters, there's a problem: your priorities are out of alignment.

If your habits are causing you to fail in areas that truly matter, it might be time to re-evaluate. Do the habits you have reflect the life you want to live? Or better yet, do the habits you have reflect the life that Christ has called you to live? If what you do is not moving you in the direction of who you want to be and who God has called you to be, is what you're doing worthwhile? What is living in the call of God for your life worth to you?

You're alive for more than just watching movies, playing video games, and wasting time on your phone. Those things aren't intrinsically bad and can be good in proper time, context, and proportion. For example, I host movie nights and game nights at my house, but it's all about connecting, relaxing, and growing as a family. However, if you isolate yourself and put all of your energy into things that don't benefit your walk with Christ and don't create a deeper connection with people, what's the point?

At the end of the day, if you're not prioritizing why you're really here, you're going to miss out. Life is so much more than just a nine-to-five job and binging Netflix. Jesus made you for more. So when the Holy Spirit speaks to your conscience and asks, "Is this the best way to be spending your time? Is this the most excellent use of your energy?", you should respond with humility.

The truth is, we don't like hearing that, do we? But why do we resist? Because of pride. Pride says, "Who are you to tell me that? Who are you to talk to me about how I spend my time?" I'll tell you who that person is: it's someone who loves you. It's someone who cares about you. It's someone who is calling you to a higher standard.

God's standard focuses on so much more than avoiding sinful things. Just because something isn't "sinful" doesn't mean that it's excellent. Remember, good is the enemy of great. When we live an excellent life, we are letting go of complacency, laziness, apathy, and mismanaged priorities. We recognize we are called to fight for the Kingdom, shining the light and life of Jesus everywhere as His valiant soldiers. The Apostle Paul exhorted us about this very thing: "No one engaged in warfare entangles himself with the affairs of this life, that he may please him who enlisted him as a soldier" (2 Tim 2:4). Why do we settle and entangle ourselves with the ordinary lifestyle of the world when we're fighting a good and noble fight on behalf of our King?

"Apathy is passionless living. It is sitting in front of the television night after night and living your life from one moment of entertainment to the next. It is the inability to be shocked into action by the steady-state lostness and suffering of the world. It is the emptiness that comes from thinking of godliness as the avoidance of doing bad things instead of the aggressive pursuit of doing good things."

- John Piper

Carpe Diem

I lead a discipleship ministry with a team of 25 leaders and volunteers, run two businesses, and maintain relationships with many people around the world. People ask me all the time how I find time to do everything I'm doing, do it with excellence, and still live with so much peace, joy, and fulfillment. One major aspect of that is the concept of *"carpe diem"* or "seize the day."

Oftentimes, we receive a new task at work, notice something that needs to be done at our house, or see an area of our relationships that is lacking attention. We set an intention in our hearts to attend to the relationship, get the task done at work, or organize our pantry, but we say, "I'll do that tomorrow." I have seen so many people slow down their progress in what God has for them to do because they simply choose to put things off until the next day. One day turns into one week, and so on. The intention they had in their heart is no more than an intention. They never allow the convictions and desires that God has placed in their life to become reality. Then they come to me and wonder why three years have passed and they haven't grown much.

Proverbs 27:1 tells us not to boast about tomorrow because we don't know what it will bring! Jesus said, "Therefore do not worry about tomorrow, for tomorrow will worry about its own things. Sufficient for the day is its own trouble" (Matt. 6:34). If you do what is set before you today, you will likely be prepared for what tomorrow brings. Today has enough complications of its own.

I often think about how what I'm doing today will affect the big picture of my life down the road. If I constantly put off maintenance on my car, problems will eventually arise. If you know anything about cars, you know that as one thing breaks, it causes other parts of the car to have to compensate. As a result, those parts wear out more quickly. If I put off the maintenance continually, my car may break down altogether and cost much more than if I had replaced the brakes as soon as I noticed them going out. The choice to take care of your responsibilities today instead of tomorrow will often save you trouble in the long run.

Proverbs says, "A little sleep, a little slumber, a little folding of the hands to rest—and poverty will come on you like a thief and scarcity like an armed man" (Prov. 24:33-34 NIV). We don't like to hear scriptures like this, but Solomon is pointing out a simple truth of life. Take care of what you can today, and don't put it off until tomorrow. Seize the day.

You may ask me, "What does this have to do with excellence?" A significant part of excellence is taking what responsibilities and opportunities God has placed before you and stewarding them well today. When you realize that God is your eternal encouragement and the source of the good things in your life, you will begin to see that you are living in a continual flow of good and perfect things coming into your life.

The ministry I lead, the businesses I run, and the phenomenal relationships I have, all began by co-laboring with God's promises. Many years ago, I received several prophetic words that I would write books about discipleship. By partnering with what God was declaring over my life, I have written many books and plan on writing many more! I did not wait for tomorrow because tomorrow will always have a new challenge that I will have to overcome. What promises have you received from the Lord for your life? How long have you left those promises on the shelf? It's time to dust them off and begin acting on them.

Stewardship

In all my years of mentoring people, one of the largest areas of lack is in the area of stewardship. I find that they may not have a clean room, car, or house. They may have poor health and or a messy appearance. My goal is not to change their external actions but to address the mindsets behind why they do what they do. Stewardship is a litmus test that reveals your understanding of God's excellence toward you in all He does. When you know the excellence of His mercy and grace, you won't be able to help but honor what you've been given by stewarding it with excellence.

The standard of cleanliness you hold often reveals how you think about yourself and how you live your life. As I have previously said, everyone has grown up in a different home with a different standard. That applies to cleanliness as well. Some of you reading this book might have grown up in a house so clean that you could've eaten food off the floor. Yet others reading this book may have last week's pizza boxes still sitting underneath the coffee table right next to a pile of half-finished soda cans.

The way you keep your house and appearance can often reveal the degree of peace you are walking in. Have you ever been so busy or overwhelmed that when you finally slowed down, you began to notice how cluttered your living space has become? This happens because when we are lacking a feeling of stability and peace internally, we tend to reveal that in the world around us.

Understand that I'm not saying things are never allowed to get messy or disorganized. We all have busy days when we don't get around to everything we want to do. However, if you find yourself continuously passing off on cleaning your room, pantry, or house, you should ask yourself why is that. What are you saying yes to at the expense of taking care of yourself and your surroundings?

Remember that we never just wake up one day and find that our lives are filled with compromise. It's always a process starting with little decisions that add up into big problems. It's "the little foxes that spoil the vines" (So. 2:15). The way you manage your house, car, workspace, clothing, and personal hygiene is a direct reflection of how well you grasp excellence. Excellence isn't about just doing what is expected of you but going above and beyond because we have an inner drive to do everything we do in a way that pleases the Lord. If we ever find ourselves reacting out of obligation, we're doing it all wrong!

Steward like Solomon

Sometimes we don't see the value of keeping things clean and organized because we don't think anyone would care or notice. However, look at the example of Solomon's life. Solomon had received wisdom from God that far exceeded any man that had ever lived. He was so wise and excellent in all that he did, and his name quickly spread throughout the ancient world.

One of the great rulers of Solomon's day was the Queen of Sheba. Upon hearing of his great wisdom, she planned a trip to go and seek his advice on the most difficult matters she could conceive. When she came to his palace, she exclaimed that the stories she had heard did not do his kingdom justice. In fact, she specifically commented about his house, servants, the clothing of his servants, the food he ate, and how he worshiped the Lord. She realized that the wisdom and excellence he walked in could not have possibly been gained simply from growing up in a good family or from having an above-average IQ. She immediately recognized that it came from the Lord of Israel, the God whom Solomon personally worshiped and revered.

It wasn't a power encounter or prophetic word that made the queen see that God was real. It was the thought and order with which Solomon ran his kingdom that led her to catch a glimpse of the One True God. Wow! Some people won't be interested in hearing what God can do in their lives until they have seen the evidence of what He has already done. Sometimes that evidence isn't anything overtly supernatural or profound but simply the order and peace we have in our inner world.

I can already hear some of the practical people asking, "So are you saying that I need to go and buy the most expensive things to show God is at work in my life?" No. I'm not saying that you need material things to showcase God's goodness. You may not have money to spend on expensive brands, but you can always afford to care about how you look. This doesn't mean we need to go out and buy the latest designer brand, but a nice pair of shoes that are well cared for says something different about you than a pair of worn-out shoes. We don't realize that every day, we are sending a message to others by how we treat ourselves and our possessions.

I spend a lot of time meeting with people at my house. Because of that, I spend hours sitting on my couch. For years, I would get used couches that were worth $200 or less, but one day it dawned on me that I spend a large portion of my life sitting on my couch. Because the way I sit affects my body and long-term health, I realized that purchasing an expensive, well-made couch was very practical and an outflow of excellence. I do not buy very nice brands to get the approval of other people, but rather, I buy nice brands because of the quality and functionality they have.

I always tell my leadership team, "I don't mind giving or spending money, but I absolutely hate wasting money." The key is value. I will spend extra money on things that are high-quality.

One of the Grace Place Ministries board members has a saying I love: "ALAPAMAIT." It stands for "as little as possible [but] as much as it takes." That's the kind of mindset I have. I will spend as much as it takes to walk in excellence, from the care of my body and the meals I eat to the supplements I take and the quality of the products I purchase.

You'd be hard-pressed to find a time where I settle for a cheap, knock-off brand or a budget airline flight. I know that in the long run, the *cost* of settling for less actually exceeds the *investment* made into a quality product. The time you spend nickel-and-diming, trying so hard to get it cheap, all fails to pay itself back. You may end up replacing the item multiple times because you settled for a lower standard, while I still have luggage and dozens of other products that have lasted for years. It's hard to beat a product, service, or piece of technology that has a good return policy, lifetime guarantee, or quality standard backed with good customer service.

Speaking of taking care of my body, I've noticed that, sadly, many people don't care about the way they smell, look, or act. I find this usually stems from a couple of places. First, many people don't see their value or worth. Part of excellence is realizing that we are valuable to God. In response to the extravagant love He has poured out on us, we should live excellently toward ourselves and others. If you treat your health, personal hygiene, and fashion sense with neglect, what kind of message does that send about how well God has loved you? God gave His very own Son to have a relationship with you. If you don't value yourself enough to treat your body and wardrobe with care, have you really experienced His love for you?

Another reason I believe people do not care about personal hygiene is that they are thinking more of themselves than they are of the people around them. As followers of Christ, we're called to prefer others above ourselves. There are many ways to do this, but a very practical way to do this is to brush your teeth, comb your hair, and put on deodorant. This may sound silly, but people really do notice how we smell and look. Taking care of your hygiene is very easy to do but also easy not to do. If you find yourself neglecting your personal care routines, consider why. It's a very practical way to show love to the people around you. Do yourself and the people you love a favor and do a quick "hygiene check" before you walk out the door!

This may be a wake-up call for you. You may look around and recognize that the way you treat your possessions or personal hygiene is not excellent. They don't reflect God's abundant love and grace toward you. Let that awareness sink into the way you think about life. Don't get condemned about it, but do make a choice to be different, and ask the Holy Spirit what He wants you to change first. You may not be able to change everything at once, but you can make the initial step and allow God to lead you.

Often, I find that it is difficult for people to change their habits because they don't change who influences them. Find someone whose standards you respect or admire and spend time with them in their environment. Continue to fill your mind with excellent things. The more you do this, the more you'll be able to notice and appreciate excellence in the world around you. The more you notice and value it, the more you'll want it in your own life.

Holy Speech

"Let there be no filthiness (obscenity, indecency) nor foolish and sinful (silly and corrupt) talk, nor coarse jesting, which are not fitting or becoming; but instead voice your thankfulness [to God]."

– Ephesians 5:4 [AMPC]

People say, "Well, Daniel, I don't feel convicted about my language." Again, the standard is not whether or not we feel conviction over something. What matters is whether or not it's right. Do you see Jesus using profanity? Do you see that in any of the disciples and apostles that followed after Him? Some might say yes, and use scriptures where Jesus and the disciples used sharp or severe sayings as justification for profanity to be acceptable.

Let me ask you this. Why is it that when a toddler or child is in the room, people have a heightened sense of the language they are using, the lyrics to songs, or the content playing on the television? If a child walked into your room right now and started shouting the F-word, you probably wouldn't think it was cute or funny. You'd most likely cringe and feel like something was wrong. Most people inherently know that some language and content are not decent or appropriate for a child. Why is that? Because they know the child has *innocence* worth protecting.

Through His blood, we have become innocent again. Scripture says that when we are born again, we become like little children (Ephesians 5:1-2, 1 Peter 1:4, 1 Peter 2:2). This means that in the same way it should feel wrong for profanity to come from the mouth of a toddler, it should feel wrong for obscene language to come from our own mouths. This passage says, "Let there be no filthiness or corrupt talk." This isn't about preference. It's about the truth. Let's look deeper at what the Word says about our language:

"But shun profane and idle babblings, for they will increase to more ungodliness."
- 2 Timothy 2:16

"Let no corrupt word proceed out of your mouth, but what is good for necessary edification, that it may impart grace to the hearers."
- Ephesians 4:29

These are clear, bold statements where God instructs us on how to live. The word used in Ephesians 4:29 for "corrupt" is the Greek word *sapros* which means "rotten" or "worthless." In other words, this verse could read, "let no rotten or worthless thing proceed out of your mouth." Isaiah 55:11 says that no word that comes out of the mouth of God returns void, always accomplishing what He desires. God has no worthless words. Every word carries purpose. If we are made in the image of God, bought with the blood of Jesus, don't you think the same is true for us?

If the Holy Spirit, who is the Spirit of God, lives inside of you, why should we speak any differently than He does? Even more importantly, if our words have the same power to create as God's do, what are we releasing into the world when we speak a foul and corrupted word? Matthew 7:18 says a bad tree can't bear good fruit. Why should we expect bad words to reap a good harvest? As the family of God, it's time to take responsibility for the words we are speaking and the consequences they have.

"Don't let anyone look down on you because you are young, but set an example for the believers in speech, in conduct, in love, in faith and in purity."

- 1 Timothy 4:12 (NIV)

Paul puts equal importance on speech as he does on conduct, love, faith, and purity. We are called to set an example in our speech. If we are confident in our calling in these other areas, we should be equally confident in our calling to speak well. Guarding our language, like many other spiritual disciplines, is just as easy *to* do as it is *not* to. We live in a world that has let many virtues slip away, but we do not have to live like the world around us. We can be an example in all areas, not just a select few. Make a commitment to guard your words with the same care you use to guard your heart. Take authority over your language and decide to only let what edifies others come from your mouth.

"Death and life are in the power of the tongue, And those who love it will eat its fruit."

- Proverbs 18:21 (NASB)

Christ is the Power to Change

Many of us are so used to living beneath the standard God sets for us in Christ that we feel living in excellence is unattainable. Some of you reading this may have had the thought, "With so much to live up to, how can we possibly achieve all this?" Some people make a big deal about not being able to do the previously mentioned things and excuse their behavior.

They think, "Well, I'm fashionably late." "I have kids, and kids are messy." "I talk how I talk." "I've been this way my whole life because that's just the kind of person I am." "I can't help it—it's in my nature." Please don't misunderstand me, I'm not talking about one-off scenarios where your child melts down or you get a flat tire. I'm talking about having a consistent habit of living below the standard.

The lie many people buy into is that they are defined by their bad habits. The fact of the matter is that is *not true*. If you think you are your habits, you're a victim of something outside of your control. But if they are separate from you, that means there is hope for change. If you step back and remember that you have the Spirit of God inside of you, you can break free of any bad habit or cycle of sin, even if you've done it your whole life. The first step to getting free from bad habits is to admit that you have a problem. Notice I didn't say admitting that *you* are the problem. If you think you *are* a "late person" or if you *are* "an alcoholic," then you will never have the power to overcome that issue. You are not the problem. Who you are is found in Christ.

Don't identify with your habits. If there are areas where you need to repent for living under a low standard, do it. Then walk away, knowing Christ has set you free from the weight of any bondage. You are not what you do. But what you do is supposed to reflect something about the character and nature of God. Don't let the world's definition of what is acceptable be acceptable for you. Live free in Christ.

Conclusion

*"It's time for the people who walk in the power of the Holy Spirit
to walk in the character of Christ."*
- *Todd White*

There once was a wise, old man who lived on top of a mountain. He had long white hair and a long white beard. At the bottom of the mountain, there was a village, and all the people in the village knew about the wise old man. Whenever the villagers had a question, they would always go up to the top of the mountain and ask the old man, and he would always have an insightful answer to give.

One day in the village, two unruly teenagers said to each other, "You know what, let's go trick this old man. He can't always have the right thing to say. He can't always know the truth in every situation. How can we do it, though?"

They put their heads together, and finally, one of them said, "I have a perfect idea! I know what we can do. Let's grab a little baby bird and keep it in our hands. When we go up, we can ask the man, 'Is the bird alive or is it dead?' and if he says 'It's alive,' we'll kill it, show him, and say, 'It's dead! You're wrong.' And if he says 'It's dead,' we'll show him and say 'No, see, it's alive.'"

So, they walked all the way up the mountain to the old man's cabin and peered in. As they knocked on the door, they saw the man, with his long, white beard and scraggly white hair, come to the door. He opened it, asking, "How can I help you?"

With the bird behind their back, the boys replied, "Wise, old man, what do we hold in our hands?"

The man could hear the bird chirping, and he said, "Judging by the sound, I say you're holding a bird."

The boys said, "Old man, surely you are the wisest of them all. Tell us, is the bird alive or is it dead?" The wise man thought, If I tell them it's alive, they'll kill it, and if I say it's dead, they'll keep it alive. He took a moment to think about how to answer the boys.

Finally, he said, "Young men, the bird that you hold in your hands is as you will it to be." The boys were shocked. The old man cut through their intentions with wisdom as sharp as a double-edged sword. He saw beyond their tricks and spoke a deeper truth.

You see, every decision in your life and in your future is as you will it to be. It can be easy to fall under the spell of victimization, allowing the world around you to dictate your decisions. However, wisdom puts the ball in your court. What are you going to do? The highest form of greatness is submitting your will to God's will. Only then will you actually see excellence on display in your life.

When Walt Disney created the movie Snow White and the Seven Dwarves in the 1930's, he was creating something the world had never seen. One of the animators, Ward Kimball, spent nearly a year and a half animating a scene of Snow White trying to teach the dwarves how to eat soup. However, when the final movie was being edited, he received the heartbreaking news that Disney had cut the scene from the film entirely.

To Walt, the scene took away from the clear communication of the story. He knew that if this was going to win the affection of Hollywood, every scene of the story mattered. The pacing of how the story would be portrayed was key. It didn't matter to him the length of time that was spent building this scene. Keeping this scene took away from the central message of the film.

Take a moment to think about the "movie" of your life. What good things is God wanting to remove from your life because it's not the main thing? Do you want to put in every possible extra scene just to have a good laugh, or do you want your life to flow in excellence with the Word and will of God in which He has called you?

As I have mentioned, when you surrendered your life to Jesus, you gave up the right to decide between right and wrong. Wrong is no longer an option. You must now decide between good, better, and best—and in actuality, good and better shouldn't be options either. The Bible calls us to be excellent in everything we do. Whatever we do, we do unto the glory of God. The pursuit of excellence is never a matter of simply choosing between what is good or bad. It is choosing what is best or superior because it will always enable us to accomplish what God has called us to do and to be.

Now, if this is true, it means that the pursuit of excellence must prompt us to change. In other words, when we pursue excellence, we learn new standards and new ways of living. When we pursue excellence, we also need to get rid of baggage: old mindsets, habits, lifestyles, and maybe even relationships.

Life comes at us like one of those moving walkways you see in airports, and you're "walking upstream" against its intended motion. So if you stop moving, you'll go backward. Steve Backlund, a mentor in my life, says it like this, "If you're not growing, you're dying." People think they can sit and camp and everything will just stay the same. This is not true. You're actually traveling backward when you don't move forward because the force of life and the things the enemy is trying to throw at you will push you that way. In my years of mentorship and pouring into young believers, I see it time and time again: you are either being discipled by Jesus or by the world. There is no in-between.

As I said earlier, the way you live your life should give people a reason to praise God. However, if you're caught up in compromise or don't "feel convicted" by committing sinful actions, what will they see that gives them a reason to glorify God? Don't be ashamed of passionately following Jesus. Don't be ashamed of your love for Him in front of other people. You don't have to care what people will say.

We're not called to please the lost—we're called to show them the reality that comes through knowing Jesus so they can be saved. You were not meant to be stagnant. You're called to run a race and finish well. That's why you have to focus on what Jesus has done; that's what sets you free. You were not made in the image of the world but in the image of God. Jesus is the desire of the nations. Represent Him well, and the world will come running to sit at His feet.

If you've never heard this message before, this book might have been very challenging for you. If you felt the conviction of the Holy Spirit as you read this book, I strongly encourage you to make a change in your life today. If you are ready to give up a life of sin, or even a life filled with "good" and "better" rather than "best" and "excellent," here is a specific prayer for you to pray out loud:

Father, I ask that Your Holy Spirit would meet me right where I am. Lead me and guide me into all truth. I ask that You would reveal to my heart and mind any area that I am not walking in excellence. I ask that you would soften my heart. I repent and ask that my mind would be renewed to the truth: You have called me to live above reproach.

You have called me to live in excellence. You have called me to make godly decisions and to represent Christ in conduct, in speech, in faith, in purity, and in everything I do.

I choose to move on from the past and embrace my new creation identity! No more settling for "good" when what is best and excellent is my portion! Let Your grace wash over me. It's time for me to elevate my standard of living to Your standards in every area.

Thank You, Holy Spirit, that You've given me the ability to live how You've called me to live. I can't do it on my own! But in my weakness, You make me strong! With the supernatural power of Christ flowing within me, nothing is impossible. Thank You, Holy Spirit, that because of You,

I can do all things. Thank You for Your mercy and Your grace. In Jesus' name, I pray. Amen.

Now, here is my prayer for you:

Father, I ask that Your peace and Your grace would come upon every person that reads this and that they would be instilled with a revelation of what actions to take. I pray that they would have a conviction of excellence that would never be driven out by their selfish desires.

God, I pray that none of us would ever be driven by any of our selfish interests but that we would be led by our union with You. I ask that we would be led by our oneness with You.

Spirit of Christ, thank You that You lead us and are able to take us where You want us to go. Thank You that You give us the words to say and that You're always there. You never leave us or forsake us—Your love is always here.

Father, I thank You for the helmet of salvation that protects our minds from the lies of the enemy that say, "You can't do this. You're not good enough. Your past prevents you from this." I thank You for the helmet of salvation to protect everyone's mind. I thank You for the shield of faith and the breastplate of righteousness, and I pray that you would instill in our hearts and minds right now the truth that we are made righteous because of what You did for us. It's not because of what we do, not because of what we have done, but because of what You have done. Thank You for the ability to walk excellently in everything we do by Your grace.

In Jesus' name, Amen.

About Grace Place

Grace Place Ministries is a discipleship community fueled by a passion to see God's people walk out their identity in Christ and establish His Kingdom upon the earth. We are committed to developing mature Christian leaders through one-on-one mentoring, building family through weekly gatherings, and providing leadership opportunities designed to facilitate connection and growth. We travel frequently to minister around the world and create resources to build up the Church in her righteous identity.

————————

Vision

Mature sons and daughters
established in their identity in Christ,
spreading the Gospel of grace and truth.

Mission

Disciple young adults.
Minister around the world.
Resource the nations.

Discipleship is our Mission; Will you Join Us?

Now, more than ever, the body of Christ needs to arise and shine. The world is searching for answers and is in need of an encounter with God's love and truth. Who will raise up a generation to bring answers our world is desperately seeking?

"For the earnest expectation of the creation eagerly waits for the revealing of the sons of God."
– Romans 8:19

Whether it is a young man or woman needing a mentor or an entire church seeking the resources to disciple their community, you can make an impact!

Become a Partner with Grace Place Ministries:

Go to:
WWW.GRACEPLACEPARTNER.COM

Grace Place Ministries

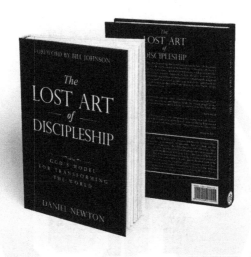

ADDITIONAL RESOURCES

THE LOST ART OF DISCIPLESHIP
Workbook

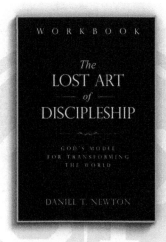

Enrich your understanding and increase your mastery of God's
model for world transformation. This companion workbook to
The Lost Art of Discipleship book is filled with exclusive content,
in-depth exercises, and practical coaching to introduce a
lifestyle of discipleship in your day-to-day walk. Whether you
have been following the Lord for years or recently surrendered
your life to Jesus, this manual breaks down the Great Commission and equips you for a life of fruitfulness!

Available at www.GracePlaceMedia.com

@GracePlaceDiscipleship

THE LOST ART OF DISCIPLESHIP
Online Course

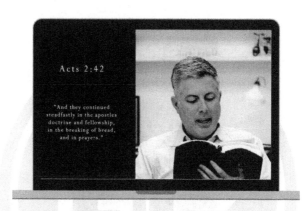

You can live the Great Commission. Every believer is called to embrace Jesus' final command: to make disciples... and this interactive online course is designed to take you even deeper into the rich content taught in *The Lost Art of Discipleship*.

Whether you are wanting to position yourself as a son or daughter, lead as a father or mother, or create a culture of discipleship, this course is for you! Rediscover the lost art with over five hours of video content, practical teaching, quizzes, and supernatural activations from Daniel Newton.

Available at www.GracePlaceMedia.com

@GracePlaceDiscipleship

ADDITIONAL RESOURCES

IMMEASURABLE
Reviewing the Goodness of God

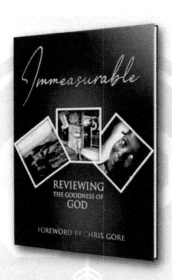

You are made in the image of the Miracle Worker,
designed to manifest His glorious nature.
Immeasurable: Reviewing the Goodness of God is a collection
of 100 real-life stories of salvation, healing, deliverance,
signs and wonders, reconciliation, and provision. Every
miracle is a prophetic declaration of what God wants to
do in, through, and for someone just like you.

Available at www.GracePlaceMedia.com
@GracePlaceDiscipleship

ADDITIONAL RESOURCES

TRUTH IN TENSION
55 DAYS TO
Living in Balance

NEVER GIVE UP
The Supernatural Power of
Christ-like Endurance

Other Titles

THE LOST ART OF PERSEVERANCE
Rediscover God's Perspective on Your Trials

ALL THINGS
Have Become New, Work Together for Good, Are Possible

IT IS FINISHED
Exposing the Conquered Giants of Fear, Pride, and Condemnation

THE LOST ART OF FAITH RIGHTEOUSNESS
Rediscover How Believing Leads to Receiving

THE LOST ART OF FASTING
Cultivating a Deeper Hunger for God

THE LOST ART OF SELFLESS LOVE
Freely Receive. Freely Give.

Available at www.GracePlaceMedia.com

@GracePlaceDiscipleship

ADDITIONAL RESOURCES

GP MUSIC: BEGINNINGS

Everyone has a story. Most people don't realize that God doesn't just want to improve their story. He wants to rewrite it. Beginnings offers a fresh start, a new focus. This worship album invites you into the core anthems of grace and truth which have impacted us at Grace Place.

Our prayer is that this album helps you lay down your past mistakes, your present circumstances, and your future worries in order to lift both hands high in surrender to the One you were created to worship. We ask that you join us in a new beginning — an exciting start to a life filled with perseverance, focus, and surrender.

Available at www.GracePlaceMedia.com

@GracePlaceDiscipleship

KEEP US UPDATED

We would love to connect with you and hear about everything God has done in your life while reading this book! We also would love to hear how we can be praying for you. Submit a testimony or prayer request by going to www.GracePlaceRedding.com/mytestimony

STAY CONNECTED WITH GRACE PLACE

Are you interested in staying up to date with Grace Place Ministries and receiving encouraging resources via email?

VISIT OUR WEBSITE:
www.GracePlaceRedding.com

SIGN UP FOR OUR NEWSLETTER AT:
www.GracePlaceRedding.com/newsletter

FOLLOW US ON SOCIAL MEDIA:
@GracePlaceDiscipleship

Made in the USA
Las Vegas, NV
21 April 2023